OUR WORLD IN COLOR

MALAYSIA

OUR WORLD IN COLOR
MALAYSIA

Photography by Ian Lloyd
Text by Wendy Moore

The Guidebook Company Limited

Distributors

Australia and New Zealand: The Book Company,
100 Old Pittwater Road, Brookvale, NSW 2100, Australia.

Canada: Prentice Hall Canada,
1870 Birchmount Road, Scarborough, Ontario MIP 257, Canada.

Hong Kong: China Guides Distribution Services Ltd.,
14 Ground Floor, Lower Kai Yuen Lane, North Point, Hong Kong.

India and Nepal: UBS Publishers' Distributors Ltd.,
5 Ansari Road, Post Box 7015, New Delhi 110 002, India.

Singapore and Malaysia: MPH Distributors (S) PTE Ltd.,
601 Sims Drive, No. 03/07-21, Pan-I Complex, Singapore 1438.

UK: Springfield Books Limited,
Springfield House, Norman Road, Dendy Dale,
Huddersfield HD8 8TH, West Yorkshire, England.

USA: Publishers Group West Inc.,
4065 Hollis, Emeryville, CA 94608, USA.

Title Spread
*Raised high above the Malacca
Straits, this traditional
fish trap, locally known as a
kelong, is silhouetted by the
setting sun off Pantai Kundor,
north of Malacca.*

Right
*A wooden fishing boat,
registered 'PP' for Pulau Pinang
(Penang), floats in the pale-
green waters off Batu
Ferringhi, Penang's most
popular beach.*

Pages 6-7
*Kuala Lumpur's futuristic
Tabung Haji building, seen
here mirrored in marble,
is the organising centre for the
annual pilgrimage to Mecca.*

Pages 8-9
*Rows of 19th-century shop-
houses are characteristic of
downtown Georgetown, the
capital of Penang state.*

Pages 10-11
*Malaysia's tropical climate
produces a kaleidoscope of
colourful flora and fauna:
geometric rows of oil palms
(top far left), glistening red
rose-apples (2nd from top
left), sweet corn and sugar cane
(mid & lower left), fan-
shaped traveller's palms (lower
far right), and a diverse
array of butterflies including
the famed black and green
coloured Raja Brooke's
Birdwing (2nd from top near
left).*

Text by Wendy Moore
Photography by Ian Lloyd

Edited by Nick Wallwork
Series Editor: Rose Borton
Photo Editor: Caroline Robertson
Artwork by Aubrey Tse, Au Yeung Chui Kwai

Printed in Hong Kong

ISBN 962-217-118-4

THAILAND

MALAYSIA

THE PHILIPPINES

SOUTH CHINA SEA

Kota Baru

Kota Kinabalu

STRAITS OF MALACCA

Penang

PENINSULAR MALAYSIA

SABAH

Cameron Highlands

BRUNEI

Gunung Mulu National Park

EAST MALAYSIA

Malacca

Mersing

SARAWAK

Kuching

SINGAPORE

INDONESIA (KALIMANTAN)

INDONESIA (SULAWESI)

INTRODUCTION

FROM HIGH in the misty mountains, legendary home of a giant serpent, the river winds like the coils of the naga itself through the overhanging jungle. Vines and creepers loop from tree to tree like the rigging of ghostly galleons and along the riverbanks, where the sunlight penetrates, flowering lianas with clusters of fiery orange blossom light up the evergreen of the jungle.

High up in the treetops, where the great trunks burst suddenly into branches, huge hanging fern-gardens bask in the sun. Whitefaced monkeys rattle the treetops and an orchestra of insect and animal life create a weird, hypnotic barrage of sound. All about are the dancing shadows, the shivering palms, the rustling foliage. In this dappled twilight of the great rainforests it is easy to imagine that the growl of distant thunder may have been a tiger's roar or that those striped shadows were its camouflaged markings. For here, deep in the Malaysian jungle where man has still to make his mark, the imagined can and does happen.

The tropical peninsula of Malaysia and her attendant states of Sarawak and Sabah, remain an enigmatic land. Although her forests may be the most ancient in the world and her encompassing seas the fabled routes of the ancient spice trade, it is still a little-known land outside of Asia. It appears that there was always an element of intrigue about Malaysia's past and the titles she inspired were just as enthralling. The Greeks knew it as the 'Golden Chersonese', the early Hindu traders called it ' The Land of Gold' and the ancient mariners coined the phrase ' The Land Where the Winds Meet'. Marco Polo called it Lokak, 'a place where gold was plentiful and where there are elephants and wild game in profusion.' But he sailed by, contending that these lands were a little too untamed. They must indeed have been wild, for this Venetian merchant was no newcomer to adventure travel.

Other tales filtered down over the ages. Stories of legendary jungle kingdoms where bejewelled rajas rode about in pomp and splendour on elephant back. But ruins of these ancient kingdoms have yet to be found. In Malaysia there is no Borobodur as in Java, no Angkor Wat like in Kampuchea but there is a wealth of literary evidence. Buddhist monks en route to India, Arab sailors and Chinese merchants, all tell of these great Malay trading kingdoms. From the evidence it appears that their buildings were of wood, but the heat and humidity, the insects and the jungle would have made short work of them aeons ago, for the rainforest is adept at obliterating mysteries. Their constructions may not have made it into the 20th century but one thing is certain—humankind has lived in these parts almost since the dawn of time. From wall paintings in Sarawak's Niah Caves and relics unearthed in Perak on the Peninsula, it can be surmised that Homo sapiens have been resident in Malaysia for at least 35,000 years.

The first traders were lured here by the bounteous gifts of the rainforest. The forest dwellers, descendants of the nomadic Borneo tribes and the orang asli, literally the 'original people' of the Peninsula, collected the prized resins, scented woods, rhinoceros horn and other exotica prized by the Chinese and Arab merchants. They traded these goods with the coastal Malays, who in turn bartered with the merchants who sailed with the trade winds to their flourishing entrepôts. For this kind of maritime trade, Malaysia was perfectly situated. The southwest winds blew the Indians and Arabs across the Bay of Bengal, while the northeasterly monsoon filled the sails of Chinese junks en route to the Malay Archipelago.

Top
Evil spirits are kept at bay by this Door-Guardian at a Penang temple; the brightly-painted locked door (above) *keeps out intruders at Malacca's 17th-century Stadthuys.*

If the existence of all the other trading kingdoms was shrouded in mystery—Malacca—the greatest Malay kingdom of all, was certainly a historic reality. Lauded by the Portuguese as 'the richest seaport with the greatest abundance of shipping that can be found in the whole world', the port city was founded in about 1400 by Parameswara, a Sumatran prince whose illustrious ancestry went back to Iskandar Zul-karnain (Alexander the Great). It was here that Malaysia recorded one of the proudest periods in her history—the Malaccan Sultanate. From those days of opulence and intellectual fertility came a wealth of literature and the genesis of today's political organization. When Parameswara converted to Islam, inspired by the influential Muslim traders from India, he became the first Sultan of Malacca and laid the cornerstone of a system of law, religion and royalty that survives to this day.

Overlooking the Straits of Malacca, on the hill now known as St Paul's, the sultans and their court enjoyed a life of medieval opulence, residing in gilded palaces, borne aloft on silk-caparisoned elephants, seated on golden thrones and waited on by scores of beautiful slavegirls. As the centre of Malay power and the most important city in Southeast Asia, Malacca drew the world's attention. The Ming Emperor of China sent his envoy Admiral Cheng Ho (the Three Jewelled Eunuch), and the Sultan reciprocated by travelling to China. Meanwhile the Portuguese, lusting to take over the Arab dominated spice trade, awaited their chance. It came in 1511 at a most opportune moment. The Sultanate was in disarray and the monarch had lost the support of the sea tribes vital for a naval battle. After their victory the Portuguese held Malacca for the next 130 years. The Dutch then wrested it from them for a further 150 years before losing it to the British. Finally, in 1957, the city reverted to Malay rule after four centuries under a foreign yoke.

Malacca's tempestuous history can be seen in its architecture. On St Paul's hill are the ruins of a church and one lone gateway—the surviving remnants of the once great 'A Famosa', the Portuguese fort. Solid as the Dutch burghers themselves are the walls of the town square, coloured a rich terracotta hue. Here sits the Stadthuys, probably the oldest Dutch building in the East, and across from this the imposing Christ Church. In the narrow maze of streets that is old Chinatown, some of the wonders of 'the town where the winds meet' are still evident. Squeezed between 18th century mosques and temples are the goldsmiths, the blacksmiths and the incense and paper-art workers, plying trades that are as ancient as the old port city itself. Although the harbour has silted up long ago, forcing the modern freighters to anchor offshore in the Straits, elegant Indonesian prahus continue to sail upriver on the prevailing winds and their mariners still barter with the Malaccan stevedores much as their ancesters did.

Malacca today is a bustling, energetic city, but when Isabella Bird, the intrepid Victorian traveller, passed through here in 1879 it was quite a different scene. She found it 'very still, hot, tropical, sleepy and dreamy . . . a town out of the running, utterly antiquated . . . a veritable sleepy hollow'.

The reason for Malacca's decline was Penang, her upstart rival further north up the Straits, the new hub of the British in the East—'The Pearl of the Orient'. Penang is still an exciting place. The allure of Asia is electric here. Travellers know it as a vacation island, situated off the northwest of the peninsula, but it is much more than that. True, it has a reputation that far outweighs its size. It has been a vivacious place from the beginning. Colonel Light, Penang's founder, tricked the Sultan of Kedah into ceding it to the East India Company. After deciding on the location for his capital, Georgetown, he encouraged the clearing of the jungle by flinging silver coins into the undergrowth. Penang has been motivated for change ever since. Today, the island leads northern Malaysia in both commerce and progress and it seems most fitting that Asia's longest bridge should connect Penang with the mainland.

Penang's beaches are still the mecca of tourists the world over, and although highrise luxury hotels loom overhead, the charm of Penang persists. Downtown Georgetown, a sea of red tiled roofs, turn-of-the-century shophouses and bazaars, temples and mosques, is still intact. One can still feel the allure of Penang that Patrick Balfour, a New Yorker, felt when he travelled here on his 'Grand Tour' in the 1930s. 'It was the first time since leaving Europe that I found a place where Europeans lived from choice.'

However, Kuala Lumpur, the present capital and undisputed hub of Malaysia, was a different story. In its early days as a rough mining settlement no-one of consequence would have thought of living there. Even the Malay chieftains, whose land the Chinese mined, chose not to live in this 'muddy estuary'—the literal translation of Kuala Lumpur. Isabella Bird, our adventurous Victorian, made a cursory reference to it, but wisely bypassed it on her way north—and that was only in 1879. At that time it was a mere trading and shanty town racked by constant battles between the opposing clans of Chinese miners. But Yap Ah Loy, the Captain Cina (Headman of the Chinese) and a self-made entrepreneur, took a gamble on this crude settlement. He ploughed some of his vice-den and opium proceeds into a hospital and a brick factory; then tin prices started to boom and Kuala Lumpur's meteoric rise began.

The English rather belatedly realized the strategic importance of moving into the Selangor interior and sent one of their rising stars, a young Frank Swettenham, to become the new British Resident. Together with Yap Ah Loy, who had straightened out the Chinese troubles, and Tengku Kudin, the Malay prince who sided with the British, Swettenham transformed the former shanty town. A phoenix rose from the ashes. Brick buildings, the symbols of prosperity, emerged, roads were constructed and enterprising businessmen and adventurers flocked in. When the railway was built from Klang harbour to Kuala Lumpur, Sultan Abdul Samad, the Malay ruler of Selangor state, took a ride and pronounced it 'the best bullock cart I have ever travelled in'.

Kuala Lumpur's star was now in the ascendant, and in 1896, less than 40 years after the first tin miners erected their rough settlement, it became the capital of the Federated Malay States. It has been in the forefront of Malaysian life ever since. In 1957 the Union Jack was lowered for the last time and the city became the capital of Independent Malaya. Later, in 1961, Tunku Abdul Rahman, the first Prime Minister, formed the Federation of Malaysia, originally planned to include Malaya, Singapore, North Borneo, Sarawak and Brunei. The latter's sultan declined: he was not about to share his substantial oil revenues; and later, in 1965, Singapore left to become a separate nation. The other territories constitute today's Malaysia, and Kuala Lumpur remains its still-growing, ever-changing capital.

Although the city's highrises dominate the skyline and new suburbs creep out

Top
A pagoda crowns Penang's Kek Lok Si Buddhist Temple, while batik-clad East Coast housewives await the bus to market (above).

Top
Symbolising 'plenty', a fish-shaped drainpipe adorns a Malaccan house, while a mythical lion decorates this Penang courtyard (above).

into the jungle-clad hills, much of KL, as the city is affectionately nicknamed, retains its history. Many of the city's earlier buildings are of an eclectic 'Moorish' architectural style. There is a domed and minareted railway station, and law courts and government offices built in this same Arabian style, giving the city a character totally unlike any other in Southeast Asia. This feeling is most evident at dusk when the muezzin's call to prayer echoes from the city's mosques, and the minarets and domes are silhouetted against a vibrant tropical sunset.

Like most cities in equatorial regions, KL really comes alive at night. Out on the streets and pavements hundreds of hawkers set up shop, peddling everything from salted fish to designer jeans. KL's multicultural, ethnic mix is in full force here. Malays, Chinese, Indians, Javanese, Eurasians and Europeans rub shoulders on the streets. Fortune-tellers and medicine men draw rapt, gullible crowds, and the delicious aroma of satay and other Malaysian delicacies waft through the sultry night air, tempting passers-by to sit down under the stars and indulge in the favourite after-work pastime—eating out.

Like most other capital cities, Kuala Lumpur also suffers from chaotic traffic and pollution, but unlike her counterparts, KL has an instant outlet—the great green heartland virtually at her back door. In the fringe suburbs, flat-dwellers have problems with mischievous monkeys and bungalow-owners have to keep their lawns trimmed, to avoid unwanted visits from passing cobras. This verdant mantle, which only a hundred years ago covered all of the Peninsula and Borneo, still blankets over two-thirds of Malaysia. Even the lands that have been cleared are still verdant, for these are the vast rubber and oil palm plantations—the agricultural wealth of the nation.

Across its mountainous spine, running from the Thai border in the North to south of Kuala Lumpur, is another totally different Malaysia; a region as far removed from the hustle and bustle of the West Coast's lively towns as can be imagined—for this is the East Coast where life goes by at a slower pace. To journey here is to travel back in time; in this unchanging place traditional lifestyles are the rule, not the exception.

From Kelantan, nestled against Thailand in the north, through Terengganu and Pahang, to Johor, the gateway to Singapore in the south, are over 700 km (435 miles) of endless golden beaches, fringed with coconut palms and lapped by the South China Sea. Every now and then, this delightful monotony is broken by an estuary or a cluster of fishermen's houses on stilts. Strung along the horizon are wooded isles encircled by coral reefs, floating in a turquoise sea. This coastline is the heartland of Malay culture, home of the bumiputra, the 'sons of the soil'—the Malays.

Unlike the West Coast, where the multiracial population reflects the Chinese and Indian influx from the English colonial days, here the Malays still dominate. The British never held sway here, for up until this century much of the Northeast Coast was under Thai suzerainty, even though this was nominal, for the states were still ruled by their own sultans. Thai overlordship often amounted to nothing more than the sending of a yearly tribute called the *bunga mas dan perak*, a small tree of exquisitely wrought silver and gold flowers. Formerly these states were totally reliant on the sea roads as their only link to the West Coast. The great mountainous interior was an obstacle only breached in the mid 20th century. With the monsoon closing all the eastern ports for three months of the year, it is little wonder that the East Coast remained so isolated and traditional. Nowhere else in Malaysia are wayang kulit (shadow puppet plays), kitemaking, woodcarving, silk-weaving and silversmithing still carried on in such timeless fashion.

Life on the East Coast has always been an intermarriage with the sea. Villages are built on stilts close to the water's edge, salt-laden winds bleach wooden homes to the colour of driftwood and fishermen park their boats under palm–thatched shelters on the beach. The coconut palms that fringe the endless shoreline are as much a part of the fishermen's lives as the sea. From the palm fronds they construct monsoon fences for protection from the relentless winds, and from their fruit comes the coconut milk and oil, the staple of their cuisine.

Paddy fields further back from the coast provide their rice, and the sea their fish—life goes on governed by the rhythms of the wind and sea as it always has. Villagers still salt their fish to provide for the long months when their boats are idle—called *musim tutup kuala*, literally 'the season when the estuaries are closed'. This is the time of the northeast monsoon when, in the past, the great junks from China, laden with silks and pearls sailed to Malacca and beyond to India and the Middle East. Some of them plied further east, stopping at the great island of Borneo, where they could find the coveted hornbill ivory and prized bezoars—stones for talismans made from the gallstones of Sarawak honeybears.

Millions of years ago, in the primeval dawn of the last Ice Age, the great jungles of Borneo and Peninsular Malaysia, now separated by the South China Sea, were one—a vast rainforest known as Sundaland. A legion of birds and beasts trooped across this landbridge but when the ice melted Borneo returned to its former isolation. Although the Malaysian Peninsula offers the jungle wilderness of Taman Negara, the National Park, nowhere has that same feeling of remoteness as the northern Borneo states of Sabah and Sarawak. Although these great jungled regions have seen their forests dwindle and traditional lifestyles all but disappear in the wake of progress, they remain one of the world's last wild horizons.

Distances here are vast. Kota Kinabalu, the capital of Sabah, is 864 km (536 miles) from Kuching (Sarawak's capital). Roads link a few of the major centres but in Sarawak, rivers are still the major form of transport. Steel-bottomed express boats (built to protect hulls from floating logs) have cut transport time down to hours, not days. Flying has reduced travelling time even more drastically. Month–long overland journeys to remote longhouses, cut off from river traffic, have been reduced to a few hours.

Seen from above, an ochre–coloured river resembling an old Chinese dragon, snakes through a carpet of trees which spreads as far as the eye can see. This serpentine maze constitutes the delta of the Sarawak River, the nucleus of Malaysia's largest state of the same name. Kuching, the capital, is another 32 km (20 miles) upstream.

This is the land of hornbills and headhunters, immortalized in Victorian literature when the hero of the day was James Brooke, an adventurous Englishman. By helping the Rajah of Brunei suppress an uprising, he was rewarded with what is now Sarawak, using Kuching as his capital. The self–styled White Rajah won over the local Dyaks and the Malays but faced greater resistance from the Iban, for their love of warfare and headhunting went contrary to Brooke's notion of

Top
East Coast vignettes: the golden domes of a Kuantan mosque and (above) *a Kelantanese top-spinner, his head wrapped in traditional batik.*

17

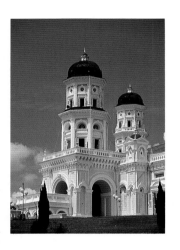

Top
Images of a multi-religious land: the Sultan Abu Bakar Mosque dominates the seafront at Johor Bahru and (above) a yellow-eyed demon glares at onlookers during Penang's Seventh Moon Festival.

Right
On the jetty at Juara, Pulau Tioman, a fisherman fills his gas-lamps for night-fishing.

government. But ultimately, with forces much greater than theirs, he defeated them.

Today, the Iban, together with the Kenyah, Kayan, Bidayan and other ethnic groups, may work in the towns and hold government positions, but upriver, many still live traditional lives in their longhouses. They grow their hill rice, fish the rivers and hunt in the jungle just as they always have done. Occasionally you may still glimpse, hanging from the centre-posts of these longhouses, a bunch of skulls, blackened with age, memories of marauding days gone by.

Sarawak may be riddled by rivers but Sabah, the 'Land Below the Wind' is dominated by mountains. Mount Kinabalu crowns the island, and at 4,101 m (13,454 feet) is not only the highest mountain in Malaysia but also the highest between New Guinea and the Himalayas. It dominates the Sabah scenery and invariably influences the traveller's agenda, for almost every visitor has its peak as their goal. Much of the climb is up near vertical staircases made of tree roots which, coupled with the heat and humidity, makes for an arduous hike.

Sir Hugh Low, a British Colonial Officer who made the first recorded climb in 1851, called it 'the most tiresome walk I have ever experienced'. Travellers today have it easy: Low had to trek from the coast before he even started the ascent. Despite the difficulties, the climb is one of Malaysia's most unique experiences. It starts in the lowland rainforest, twisting through oak, rhododendron and conifer forests, then rises up amongst the clouds to the alpine meadows and stunted bushes of the summit zone. Through these realms the lucky climber may spot the carnivorous pitcher plants, delicate orchids, flaming rhododendron forests, or be assaulted by the nauseating odour of the rafflesia—the world's largest flower. Reaching the great granite summit at dawn, just as a pink sunset breaks over Sabah, is a moving and spiritual experience. It brings to mind a quote from a tropical traveller last century, which in today's world seems harder than ever to realize. 'It is a humbling experience, and surely a healthy one, to twist to his own purposes.' And this is really something Malaysia still has in abundance; whether in a hide deep in the National Park awaiting the approach of a wild animal at a salt lick, or way upriver in the Sarawak jungle, or even while downtown in Kuala Lumpur, it is gratifying to know that out there in those limestone hills to the north of the city are miles of still untouched wilderness.

Isabella Bird remarked that Malaysia in 1879 was a *terra incognita* and she didn't only mean the jungle. Today the country is still relatively unknown and the visitor can expect a wealth of surprises: a lion dance may wind past you in Penang's back lanes; you may catch an Indian wedding at a KL temple; swim with a turtle on the timeless East Coast, or at the end of the day watch the sun go down over a silhouetted minaret while the muezzin calls the faithful to prayer. In Malaysia it's not only the jungle that is still mysterious.

Malaysia's people reflect their multi-cultural backgrounds: a Malaccan-Chinese funeral band pause for a break (top left); *a leather-clad rocker 'hangs out'* (bottom far left); *a beauty queen dazzles* (bottom left near); *Indian dancers await backstage* (top right); *Malay girls sing praises to Allah at a Koran reading contest* (mid right), *but all come together for the National Day parade* (mid left).

Eating out is a passion; whether breakfasting on 'dimsum' delicacies in Malacca (top left); buying rojak, a spicy salad from a Penang street hawker (top right); enjoying roast duck in Malacca (bottom far left), or just snacking on pickles (near left); Chinese New Year cakes (near right), or savouring the exotic array of tropical fruits (far right).

Chinese opera, locally known as **wayang**, is still enacted for all major festivals. Travelling troupes of players faithfully reproduce these musical performances dating from the classical Chinese courts of old. Trained from an early age (top right), these young girls play minor roles and will one day take over from the bejewelled leading lady (left).

Sport may well be the most popular contribution of the colonial English. Players thunder up the field in a Penang polo match (top); Ipoh footballers practice against the decorated backdrop of the Indian mosque (left); and cricketers go through their paces at the Royal Selangor Club in the heart of Kuala Lumpur (bottom).

Surrounded by feathery oil-palms, golfers tee off at the Hyatt Saujana (top right) while a lone jockey takes his racehorse for an early morning gallop (below). In Penang's annual Grand Prix a motorcyclist leans into a corner along the historic Esplanade (far right).

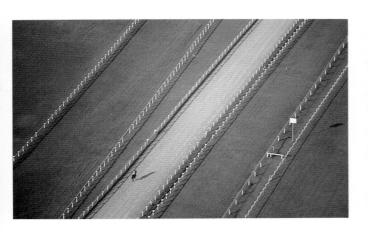

Kite-flying and top-spinning, traditional Malay games that date from the 15th century Malaccan Sultanate, still flourish on the East Coast. Measuring up to three metres wide, these kites known as wau, are made of split bamboo frames covered with decorative paper cutouts(left and top).

Strength and skill are vital prerequisites in top-spinning (right and above), for the gasing, or top, often weighs five kilograms and experienced players keep their tops spinning for two hours.

Although factories churn out mass-produced consumer goods, work by hand is still an integral part of the Malaysian way of life. In Teluk Intan, bunches of dried nipah palm leaves (above) are cut and used as paper for traditional hand-rolled cigarettes. In Kelantan (left) a craftsman chisels away at a wood carving; a Penang calligrapher (top right) writes a lucky New Year message; a Malay girl paints on a silk batik (top & mid right); and shadow puppets flicker across a lamp-lit screen re-enacting a centuries old drama (lower right).

Tourism, Malaysia's fastest growing
industry, has spawned a glittering
array of luxury hotels including
the Golden Sands at Penang (left),
the Hyatt Kuantan (below),
the Malacca Village Resort (mid &
lower far right), and the architectural
award-winning Tanjung Jara Resort
(bottom). Old time travellers, like

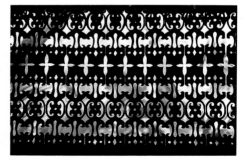

novelist Somerset Maugham, had to be content with the spartan accommodation at the Malacca Club, now the Proclamation of Independence Museum (right), *but Penang's elegant E & O Hotel* (bottom left) *still offers accommodation with old world charm.*

Seafood is an everyday feature on Malaysian tables. Early morning fish markets (top) offer the day's catch fresh from the sea and prepared into tangy dishes it is served up to discerning patrons at Malacca's Portuguese Square (left).

At a Kuala Lumpur night market, squid
are displayed for the appraisal of diners
(top right); a Penang street sign advertises
a local speciality (top left); a Portuguese-
Eurasian girl spreads salted fish to dry
on racks (mid left); and fish cakes and
other breakfast treats are displayed in
a bamboo steamer in a Malaccan coffee
shop (bottom left).

Jungle still covers 70 percent of Malaysia, but large scale clearing for plantations is fast depleting that percentage. Seen from the air, a serpentine river in Sabah, East Malaysia (right), is clouded with silt from upriver logging. In Peninsula Malaysia, much of the original coastal forest has been taken over by rubber plantations (below). Versatile bamboo (bottom) thrives in this lush climate and quickly overtakes man-made clearings.

Moorish style, 19th century architecture pervades the heart of Kuala Lumpur, where the railway station is festooned with domes and cupolas (above and left). Spotlit in the background is the minaret of the National Mosque (above).
The spectacular Tabung Haji (right) tower pierces the city skyline—a fusion of Islamic styles and contemporary design.

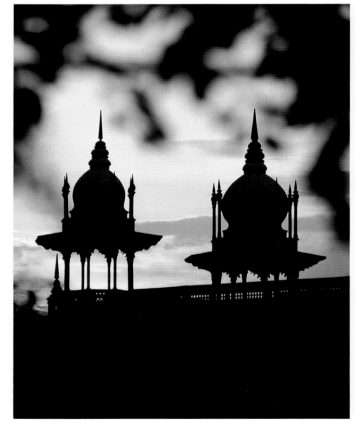

Kuala Lumpur's ethnic mix is mirrored in its architecture. Left top is the Middle-Eastern inspired Centre for Islamic Studies; far left is the colonnaded corridor of the early 20th century Railway Administration building; and across the road (near left), the setting sun outlines the flamboyant roof of the Railway station. In Chinatown (top right), traditional New Year papercuts enliven the wall of a shop-house and winged griffins (bottom right), souvenirs of the city's colonial past, decorate the base of a downtown fountain.

Malaysia's capital, Kuala Lumpur, is one of Asia's fastest growing cities. Skyscrapers sprout like mushrooms (top left), but many of the city's historical buildings remain. Sunlight strikes the copper domes of the Sultan Abdul Samad building (right) and arched verandas characterise these colonial offices (above), surrounded by buildings of a less gracious age.

The cooler air of the highlands drew the colonial English to the Cameron Highlands where they built Tudor style retreats (lower far right) and hotels like Ye Old Smokehouse (top left) which still carries on the traditions of English country life. Tea plantations were carved from the jungle (top right) and labourers were imported from India and Sri Lanka (lower right), but the Peninsula's original inhabitants, the Orang Asli, still dwell nearby in their split bamboo dwellings (lower left), torn between their traditional rainforest life and the lure of the modern world.

Kedah, in the far north of the Peninsula, is known as the 'rice bowl of Malaysia' (top left). Shaded by conical hats, women do much of the planting (bottom left), but men do the heavier tasks like threshing (near left). Although times have changed and irrigation now makes two crops a year a reality for many farmers, the life-styles of most Kedah country folk are still ruled by the rhythms of the rice season.

Ipoh, the capital of Perak state and Malaysia's newest proclaimed city, was built on mining profits, for the surrounding Kinta Valley has the world's richest tin deposits. Besides tin, Ipoh is famous for its Buddhist cave temples (near right), tucked into the nearby limestone hills. Downtown, the city advertises its colonial past at the FMS Bar (lower right), a popular watering-hole for thirsty footballers (top) training at the nearby padang, the local term for a 'playing field'.

Pilgrims and curious tourists must make an arduous ascent up 272 steps to reach Batu Caves (top left), sacred for Malaysia's Hindus. Stalactites hang from the limestone roof of Cathedral Cave, where there is a shrine to Lord Subramanian (bottom left). In Penang, the only funicular railway in Malaysia climbs 830 metres (2,723 feet) to the summit of Penang Hill (above), and a Chinese gateway frames the entry staircase of the nearby Kek Lok Si Temple (top right).

Taoism, Confucianism, and Buddhism thrive in Penang, where two-thirds of the population is Chinese. At the Kuan Yin Temple (above), believers burn joss sticks for their daily worship. At the elaborately decorated Khoo Kongsi Clanhouse (top right), scores of inscribed ancestral tablets honour the dead (top left) and porcelain dragons cavort on the tiled roof, reputed to weigh 25 tons (lower right).

One of the reasons Penang was chosen as a settlement by the 18th century English was because of its excellent deep water port. Ferries (top left) ply across the straits from Butterworth, but the new Penang bridge (above), the longest in Asia, provides a road link with the mainland. This prosperous port, fuelled by duty free status and tin and rubber exports spawned some grandiose architecture (middle & lower left), but in the quiet fishing villages of the north coast (lower right), life goes on much the same as it has for decades.

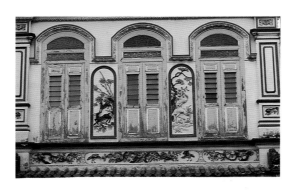

Nowhere is the past preserved as well as in 600-year-old Malacca. In Chinatown, under a sea of red-tiled roofs (top & middle right), are rows of Chinese shop-houses (lower near left) decorated with bas-reliefs (top left) and ancient temples (lower far left). Along narrow Jonker Street where trishaws still ply (mid left), antique shops abound (lower right) — a showcase of the city's six centuries of history.

Red is the colour of Malacca; from the stately 16th century walls of the Dutch-built Stadthuys (far left & mid right), a favourite venue for newly-weds (top right), to the adjacent Post Office (top left), Christ Church and Clocktower (lower left). This colour, a Chinese favourite symbolising prosperity, is echoed in devotees' candles at a religious goods shops (mid left) on a display of wooden clogs (far right), and on the pillars and decor of the Cheng Hoon Teng, Malacca's oldest Chinese Temple (near lower right).

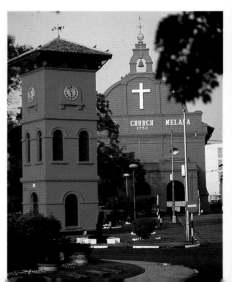

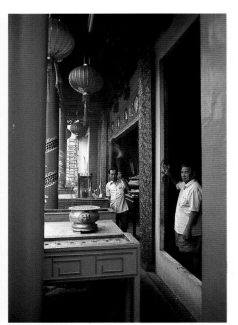

55

Every state has its own variation of the traditional Malay house, but only in Malacca are these unique tiled staircases found. Each house utilises different colours and tiles (right), but none is as splendid as the entrance to Penghulu's house at Merlimau (below) where art-nouveau designs create a dazzling effect.

57

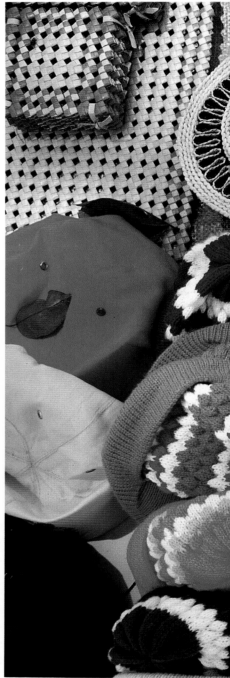

Air travellers to Pulau Langkawi, a group of 99 islands in the northwest, are treated to this spectacular sight (top), whilst those entering by road from Singapore must cross the one kilometre-long causeway (lower) which links with Johor Bahru, Malaysia's most southerly city.

Port Dickson, the closest beach to Kuala Lumpur, offers tranquil sands, where fishing boats beach at low tide (bottom right) and a large array of souvenirs. The colourful conical items in the centre are not some bizarre headgear but woven food covers!

59

Idyllic deserted beaches and a tiny offshore islet (right) *characterise Pulau Tioman, the largest island off Malaysia's East Coast. Although discovered by the tourists trade only recently, the island had long been known to sailors on the spice route as a peaceful anchorage, and for its abundant timber and fresh water* (bottom). *An island youth strums a guitar at quiet Juara on the less accessible east coast* (below).

Dozens of tropical isles lay off the coast of Johor state. On Pulau Rawa (bottom & right) it is hard to believe that a first-class resort is concealed behind the coconut palms (below). The island's pure white coral sand and clear waters make it a favourite weekend getaway for mainlanders, Singaporeans and tourists alike.

On the east coast, life still centres around the sea. In the fishing village of Marang (top left), coconut palms shade thatch-roofed huts, and further down the coast at Beserah, a carved wooden egret, known as a bangau (above), protects the fishermen from the fickle fancies of the South China Sea. At Pantai Batu Buruk, Kuala Terengganu's popular beach, a jogger enjoys the tangy sea air while a motor-cyclist snacks on a Penang-inspired noodle dish from a roadside hawker (lower left).

LAKSA
PENANG

Graceful coconut palms, long white beaches and peaceful fishing villages hug the coast north of Kuantan (top right) *where countless bays are lapped by the South China Sea* (above). *A sarong-clad fisherman tidies up his* kolek, *a traditional wooden fishing craft with curved bow and stern* (lower right). *Boat design has changed little over the centuries but sails have been replaced by more efficient outboard motors.*

Linking both sides of the Peninsula, the
East/West Highway in northern Malaysia
(above), traverses the main mountain range
providing sweeping views of the rainforest
canopy (right). Coloured trees are those
which are flowering or budding. Each
species has its own season, unlike trees
in temperate zones which share the same
season. Dominating the jungle near Batu
Melintang is Gunung Reng (left), a
limestone massif pitted with caves
believed to be the dwelling place of
Stone Age people.

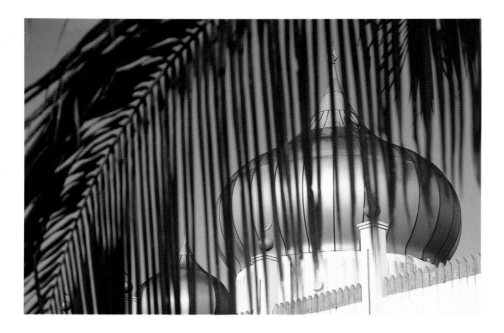

SOMU KELINIK

SOMU
சோமு
لامب
蘇母

KELINIK
கிளினிக்
جوج
藥店

Islamic design shows its influence in the palm-fringed mosque near Kuantan (top left); in Kota Bharu's octagonal market (mid left); government offices (lower left) and the town clock tower (top). At a Teluk Intan clinic (above), a bamboo blind advertises in four different languages.

Kuala Terengganu, one of the East Coast's oldest ports, hugs the boat-filled estuary of the Terengganu River (bottom right). Shuttered and carved windows (top right) decorate the shophouses of old Chinatown which cluster along the riverbank (mid right).

Sarawak, Malaysia's biggest state in the great jungled island formerly known as Borneo, is home to many races, but the native Ibans number more than 30 percent of the population. Rivers are the roads of East Malaysia (above right); and Ibans learn their water skills from an early age (upper left).
A tribeswoman manoeuvres her dugout (mid right) upriver to the longhouse where families live in communal style (lower right). On an upraised veranda, a grandmother winnows rice (lower left); and elders display their ceremonial finery including headdresses of hornbill and eagle feathers.

Before the coming of the Europeans, Sabah in Borneo's far north, was already under the influence of Islam, for the coastal regions had long been allied with the Sultanate of Borneo. Crescent moons decorate a town mosque (above) and at the State Mosque in Kota Kinabalu a large dome surmounts the smaller prayer domes (left).

A symbol of the state's development, the circular tower of the Sabah Foundation Building soars above Kota Kinabalu, the state capital (right).

At dusk, the Sarawak River near Kuching (middle) takes on a silvery glow. Sarawak's capital is home to the contemporary State Mosque (top) and the colonial fort Margherita built in 1841 (lower).

Sabah's tourist attractions include
Mount Kinabalu (top), *the highest
mountain in Southeast Asia; the
water villages of Mengkabong*
(middle), *home of the sea-roving
Bajau; and the offshore islands
of the Tunku Abdul Rahman
National Park* (bottom).

Dominating Sabah is Mount Kinabalu (left), a granite massif rising an awesome 4, 101 metres (13, 454 feet). At Tenom, the indigenous Muruts live in split bamboo longhouses (bottom) and raise water buffalo—cooling off in a mud hole (below).

In a country market square a young Sabahan (left) makes sure this chicken will make it to the cooking pot.

Following pages
Manicured tea bushes blanket the slopes 1,524 metres (5,000 feet) up at the Sungai Palas Tea Estate in the Cameron Highlands.

Page 80
A golden sunset silhouettes this yacht off Batu Ferringhi, Penang.

A

ABC Not the alphabetic variety but an abbreviation of *air batu chendol*. This popular delicacy of shaved ice topped with cream, syrup, jelly and sweetcorn is served in restaurants and on street corners throughout Malaysia.

Air Travel Apart from the national carrier, Malaysia Airlines, 27 other international airlines fly to Malaysia. International airports are situated at Kuala Lumpur and Penang in Peninsular Malaysia, at Kota Kinabalu in Sabah and at Kuching in Sarawak. Malaysia Airlines' domestic service flies to all major towns.

B

Baba and Nonya A popular term for the menfolk (baba) and the women (nonya) of the Straits Chinese, a unique ethnic minority of Malaysian Chinese. Under British rule, thousands of Chinese emigrated to Malaysia to work the tin mines and the Indians came to work as coolie labour on the rubber plantations.

Bomoh A traditional medicine man, believed to possess special healing powers. The bomoh performs religious rites in villages and is often hired to keep rain away on special occasions. Some sultans still retain a royal bomoh for ceremonial events.

Bumiputra Literally means 'sons of the soil' and is the term used to describe the Aborigines, Malays and related groups whose cultural affinities are indigenous to the region. They include the Malays, the Bajau of Sabah, the Bugis, Minangkabau, Javanese and Boyanese. These people of Malay descent share a common culture and above all the bond of Islam.

C

Cameron Highlands The queen of Malaysia's hill resort in northwest Pahang state, the Cameron Highlands rise to 1,524 m (5,000 ft) above sea level. The Highlands are famous for tea growing, colonial-style bungalows, jungle walks and vegetable farms.

Cicak Cicak is the Malay name for the ubiquitous gecko. Pronounced 'chinkchuck', the name describes the reptile's call. Some people believe that when you hear its call, someone is talking about you. Another tale relates that the reason a cicak stops before jumping on a fly is so that it has time to pray to Allah.

Climate Malaysia's climate is hot and humid with the mercury hovering between 20° to 30°C (68° to 86°F) all year round. The Northeast monsoon brings heavy rain to the East Coast, Sarawak and Sabah from December to February. The highlands are noticeably cooler and on the Mount Kinabalu summit trail, temperatures can drop to 2°C (36°F).

D

Durian The undisputed king of Malaysian fruits. The obnoxious sewer–like smell puts off many first timers, but once you have sampled the creamy rich pulp, addiction is sure to follow.

E

East Malaysia This is the name given to the Malaysian states of Sarawak and Sabah in the north of the island formerly known as Borneo. Sarawak and Sabah joined the Federation of Malaysia on 16 September 1963. The remainder of the island is taken up by Kalimantan which belongs to Indonesia.

G

Gasing Spinning the *gasing* or top spinning is a well loved East Coast sport with competitions held regularly between neighbouring Kelantanese villages. The tops, weighing approximately 5.5 kg (12 pounds), are polished, streamlined works of art about the size of a dinner plate. In a competition the person whose top spins the longest is the winner— spectators need a great deal of patience though, as the gasing has been known to spin for as long as two hours!

Gunung Mulu National Park This spectacular national park is situated in the far north of Sarawak. Within its 52,866 hectares (130,631 acres) is Gunung Mulu, a sandstone mountain 2,376m (7,795 ft) high containing a huge system of limestone caves. Clearwater Cave is 52 km (32 miles) long and the Sarawak Chamber, thought to be the largest in the world, is the size of 16 football pitches.

H

Hari Raya The Muslim festival at the end of Ramadhan, the fasting month, when the Malays 'run amok on food'. The day begins with prayers at the mosque and ends with open–house festivities where family and friends join each other for a celebratory feast.

I

Iban The Iban are the largest tribal group in Sarawak where they live beside the major rivers in their communal longhouses. A warlike tribe, the Iban were immortalized as Borneo's fearless headhunters. Today they grow hill rice and pepper and many work in Kuching.

J

Johor Johor, the most southerly state of Malaysia, is best known for its vast oil and rubber plantations and its easterly offshore islands. Its capital is Johor Baru, the gateway town to Singapore.

K

Kain Songket This silk brocade, shot with gold and silver threads, is woven by village women on the East Coast. Once the perogative of royalty, the kain songket is now popular for weddings and formal wear.

Kenduri A Malay feast held for weddings and other special occasions when the entire village, friends and relatives are invited to join in the festivities.

Kota Baru Kota Baru is the capital of Kelantan state, in the far northeast of Malaysia. A centre for traditional crafts and the performing arts, Kota Baru is the heartland of Malay culture. Pantai Cinta Berahi, 'The Beach of Passionate Love', is the most famous of the nearby beaches.

Kota Kinabalu Originally known as Jesselton, the town was razed in the Second World War but re–emerged as the capital of Sabah. Its superb geographical setting, with offshore tropical islands and a backdrop of jungle-clad hills, makes it a popular tourist resort.

Kuching Kuching is the capital of Sarawak. Legend has it that the

'White Rajah', James Brooke, named it after the Malay for cat, when this animal interrupted a meeting between him and the tribal chiefs.

L

Low Sir Hugh Low was a British Colonial Officer who made the first recorded ascent of Mount Kinabalu in 1851. During his trek he collected a variety of plant life and modestly named them after himself! Hence, trekkers on the Mount Kinabalu trail can find Low's Pitcher Plant and Low's rhododendron.

M

Makan Angin Literally 'eating the wind'. A popular term used to describe 'taking a holiday' or just 'taking it easy'.

Murut The Murut, or 'hill people', live in the hilly border regions between Sarawak and Sabah. They are shifting cultivators and excel at hunting and gathering jungle produce. The last of the Borneo peoples to give up headhunting, the Murut still hunt with a blowpipe.

Merbuk A dove prized for its song. Their bamboo cages are raised on poles high above the ground, for there they sing the sweetest. Bird-singing contests are held all over the country but are particularly popular in Kelantan.

N

Negri Sembilan Negri Sembilan means 'nine states' and refers to the nine states under different Malay rulers that were federated in 1773. Negri Sembilan's population has its

origins in the Minang Kabau of Sumatra who settled here in the 16th century. The Minang Kabau have retained their traditional houses which have upswept roofs, symbolic of the horns of the 'kabau' or water buffalo.

P

Pitcher Plants These carnivorous oddities of the plant world thrive in the cloud forests of Malaysia. Shaped like pitchers full of liquid, these plants live on the nutrients of drowned, dissolved insects. This ingenious system allows them to thrive in poor soil.

Penan Also called the Punan, these are Malaysia's only true nomadic people. Based in East Malaysia, some have now settled elsewhere, but the majority prefer to live off the jungle. These skillful hunters and craftsmen have been in the forefront of a protest against logging in order to save their indigenous lifestyle from extinction.

Population Estimated at 16.5 million (1988), Malaysia is a multi-racial society comprising: Malays, 47 percent; Sabah/Sarawak Bumiputras, 12 percent; Chinese, 31 percent; Indians, 8.5 percent and others 1.5 percent.

R

Rafflesia The world's largest flower, named after Stamford Raffles the founder of Singapore, who found it in Sumatra, its only other home besides Malaysia. This fleshy parasitic plant takes months to produce a single bloom, 45 cm (18 inches) across, which wilts within four days

Rambutan This fruit is a favourit

among visitors and is often described as a 'Hairy Cherry'. The name rambutan comes from the Malay word *rambut* meaning 'hair'. The peel turns from green to yellow and then to red as the fruit ripens.

Rantau Abang Is the East Coast beach where every year the giant leatherback turtles return to lay their eggs. June to September is the peak nesting season and the best time for viewing is at night on a high tide. People used to build fires and and listen to music while they waited for the turtles, but these activities scared them away. Luckily, the Malaysian authorities took steps to prevent this sort of behaviour and the nesting is now carefully controlled.

S

Satay Malaysia's equivalent of the hamburger. Cubes of meat, marinated and barbecued on bamboo skewers, they are usually served with a peanut sauce.

Semangat A vital force, or the soul of life, which many Malays believe exits in both man and objects. Certain jungle trees that loom above a village are never cut down for fear that someone will fall sick, and a stretch of young forest where a *pontianak* (the ghost of a woman who died in childbirth) still haunts, is never visited after dark.

Songkok A songkok is the velvet fez-like cap worn by Malay men. Songkok haji is the small white circular cap traditionally worn by those who have made the pilgrimage to Mecca.

T

aman Negara Taman Negara

National Park spreads over 4,343 sq km (1,676 sq miles) of Peninsular Malaysia. Within its boundaries are dense rainforests, fast-flowing jungle rivers, an abundance of game and the Peninsula's highest mountain, Gunung Tahan.

Tasek Cini A group of freshwater lakes in Pahang state. Legend tells of a walled Khmer city surrounded by lotus ponds that once existed hereabouts. Apparently, when an enemy tribe attacked, the inhabitants used a system of aqueducts to submerge the city in water, thus forming Lake Cini. The lake and its lotuses have been there ever since. A Loch Ness–type monster is also said to guard the depths. Apparently the serpent–like monster has two horns, a head 'as big as a tiger's' and blazing red eyes.

V

Visa Requirements Commonwealth citizens (except those from India) need no visa to enter Malaysia. Most other nations do not require a visa for a visit not exceeding three months. On entry, visitors can obtain a one-month visit pass which is free and renewable.

W

Wau The Malaysia name for a kite. Kite flying is still popular on the East Coast and competitions are held at both national and international level. A legend from Kedah links kite–flying with padi cultivation. The legend tells of a poor, childless padi farmer who came upon a little girl in his field and decided to adopt her. She grew up to be a beautiful woman and the farmer, who had bountiful harvests, doted on her so much that one day his jealous wife

beat her. The girl disappeared with the western wind and the next season the crops failed. After consulting a fortune teller, who explained that the girl was a *semangat padi*—guardian spirit of the rice field—the farmer was told to appease her by making a mythical being in the form of a kite and flying it with a string of rhea grass. Having done this, the spirit was appeased and the bountiful crops returned.

Wayang Kulit Wayang kulit literally means 'shadows made from skin' and refers to the traditional Malay shadow puppet play performed in the northern states of Kelantan, Kedah and Terrengganu. The favourite puppet play is the 2,000 year old Indian epic, *The Ramayana*. Prince Rama is still the hero, but his two Malay followers Pa' Dogol and Wak Long provide the comedy. The latter two figures were invented by a Malay puppeteer over 100 years ago.

INDEX